Roman Britain

AF435829

While every precaution has been taken in the preparation of this book, the publisher assumes no responsibility for errors or omissions, or for damages resulting from the use of the information contained herein.

ROMAN BRITAIN

First edition. April 26, 2024.

Copyright © 2024 History Nerds.

ISBN: 979-8227414465

Written by History Nerds.

Also by History Nerds

Ancient Empires
The Ottoman Empire
Rome: The Rise and Fall
The Mongol Empire
The Assyrian Empire
Ancient Egypt

Celtic Heroes and Legends
Celtic History
William Butler Yeats: Nobel Prize Winning Poet
Robert the Bruce
Scáthach
Finn McCool
William Wallace: Scotland's Great Freedom Fighter

Frauen des Krieges
Boudica: Königin der Icener
Jeanne d'Arc

Irena Sendler

Great Wars of the World
World War 1
World War 2
The Napoleonic Wars: One Shot at Glory
The Serbian Revolution: 1804-1835
Peace Won by the Saber: The Crimean War, 1853-1856
The American Civil War

Pirate Chronicles
Grace O'Malley: The Pirate Queen of Ireland
Blackbeard
William Kidd
Ching Shih
Anne Bonny

The History of England
Roman Britain
Medieval England
The Wars of the Roses
Tudor England

The History of the Vikings

Vikings
Longships on Restless Seas

Women of War
Boudica: Queen of the Iceni
Joan of Arc
Irena Sendler
Virginia Hall
Queen Amanirenas
Women of War Omnibus: Books 1-5

World History
The History of the United Kingdom
The History of Ireland
The History of America
The History of Scotland
The History of Wales
The History of India

Standalone
Grace O'Malley: Die Piratenkönigin von Irland

Table of Contents

Introduction

In the annals of history, few epochs have captured the imagination and scholarly interest as intensely as that of Roman Britain. This period, filled with conquests, cultural exchanges, and conflicts, stands as a testament to the complexity of human civilization and its propensity for both dominion and integration.

Our journey into the heart of Roman Britain aims not merely to recount the events that transpired but to delve into the undercurrents that shaped these happenings. Why did the mighty Roman Empire, with its vast territories stretching from the arid sands of Egypt to the misty lands of Scotland, set its sights on Britain? What ensued when Roman organizational prowess and military might met the fierce independence of the Celtic tribes? These questions and more lie at the core of our exploration.

As we traverse through the annals of Roman Britain, beginning with the audacious invasion of 43 AD, we are not merely recounting military campaigns and administrative maneuvers. We seek to uncover the human dimension of this historical episode—the aspirations, fears, and daily lives of those who lived through it. How did the introduction of Roman governance, infrastructure, and economic systems transform the societal landscape of Britain? In what ways did the cultural fabric of the province evolve, reflecting a confluence of Roman and Celtic influences? The chapters that follow promise a comprehensive examination, not just of battles and politics, but of the social, economic, and cultural ramifications of Roman rule.

The narrative arc of our investigation will carry us from the tumultuous conquests and rebellions, through the intricate process of Romanization, to the monumental legacy of Hadrian's Wall. Each chapter, meticulously researched and vividly portrayed, aims to offer a window into the lived experience of both the conquerors and the conquered. By examining the daily lives under Roman rule, the economic undertow of occupation, and the profound cultural exchanges that occurred, we will attempt to piece together a Roman Britain that is as rich in detail as it is broad in scope.

Furthermore, our inquiry does not halt at the decline of Roman power but extends to the enduring legacy of Rome in the British Isles. How did the withdrawal of the Roman legions influence the subsequent historical trajectory of Britain? In what ways do the imprints of Roman law, language, architecture, and governance continue to resonate within British society? The final chapters aim to bridge the historical chasm between the past and the present, illustrating the indelible marks left by Roman Britain on the collective memory and identity of the nation.

In embarking on this intellectual odyssey, dear reader, you are invited to question, reflect, and engage with the past in a manner that illuminates not only the historical landscape of Roman Britain but also the broader contours of human history. What lessons can we glean from the Roman experience in Britain that might inform our understanding of empire, culture, and identity? As we peel back the layers of history, let us ponder the ways in which the past continues to shape our present and future. Welcome to a journey into Roman Britain—a saga of power, resilience, and transformation.

Conquest and Settlement

A Timeline of Events

Firstly, before we dive into the deeper analysis of cultural synthisis that occurred between the Romans and native tribes of Britain, we want to lay out a timeline of events to set the stage for our examination.

Pre-Roman Context

Before the Romans, Britain was inhabited by various Celtic tribes, each with its own territory and leadership. These tribes included the Iceni, Trinovantes, Catuvellauni, and Brigantes. The Celtic Britons practiced agriculture, metallurgy, and trade, and their society was organized into tribal kingdoms. They constructed hill forts for defense and as centers of political power. The Druids played a significant religious and social role, serving as priests, teachers, and judges. Although there were no written records from this period, archaeological finds provide insights into their way of life, culture, and interactions with continental Europe.

Roman Conquest and Early Rule

Julius Caesar's expeditions in 55 and 54 BC marked the beginning of Roman interest in Britain, though they did not result in permanent occupation. The full-scale invasion ordered by Emperor Claudius in 43 AD, led by Aulus Plautius, brought significant parts of Britain under Roman control. Key victories included the capture of Camulodunum (Colchester), which became the first Roman capital of Britain. By 47 AD, the southeastern regions were fully subdued. The early period saw military consolidation and the establishment of Roman infrastructure, including roads and forts, which facilitated further expansion and control over the native population.

60-61 AD: Boudicca's Revolt

Boudicca, the widowed queen of the Iceni tribe, led a significant uprising against Roman rule after the Romans confiscated her lands and mistreated her family. Her forces attacked and destroyed Roman settlements including Camulodunum, Londinium (London), and Verulamium (St Albans), killing thousands of Roman civilians and soldiers. The revolt posed a serious threat to Roman authority but was ultimately crushed by the Roman governor, Gaius Suetonius Paulinus, in a decisive battle. Despite its failure, Boudicca's revolt remains a symbol of resistance against oppression and highlighted the tensions between the Roman occupiers and the native tribes.

Expansion and Consolidation

Governor Agricola's tenure from 71 to 84 AD marked a period of significant expansion. Agricola pushed Roman boundaries into modern-day Scotland, culminating in the Battle of Mons Graupius around 83 AD, where the Romans claimed victory over the Caledonian tribes. The construction of Hadrian's Wall began in 122 AD under Emperor Hadrian, establishing a defined northern frontier. This was followed by the building of the Antonine Wall in 142 AD, though it was abandoned within two decades. These efforts represented Rome's strategic defense and consolidation of power, aiming to control movement and trade, and deter invasions from northern tribes.

180-190 AD: Peace and Prosperity

The late 2nd century saw a period of relative peace and economic prosperity in Roman Britain. The establishment of towns (coloniae and municipia), such as Londinium, Eboracum (York), and Verulamium, fostered urban development and trade. Roman Britain became known for its villas, baths, and temples, showcasing a blend of Roman and local architectural styles. Agriculturally productive lands and efficient road networks facilitated trade within the province and with the wider Roman Empire. This period also saw the growth of a Romano-British elite, who adopted Roman customs, language, and governance, contributing to the stability and prosperity of the region.

196 AD: Clodius Albinus

Clodius Albinus, the governor of Britain, declared himself emperor in 196 AD amidst the political turmoil following the assassination of Emperor Pertinax. Aligning initially with Septimius Severus, Albinus later turned against him, claiming the imperial title for himself. In 197 AD, Albinus crossed into Gaul with his legions to confront Severus but was defeated at the Battle of Lugdunum (modern Lyon, France). His defeat led to Severus consolidating his power as emperor. This period highlighted the strategic importance of Britain and its legions in imperial power struggles, demonstrating the province's critical role in the wider Roman Empire.

208-211 AD: Septimius Severus in Britain

Emperor Septimius Severus launched a military campaign in Britain in 208 AD to subdue rebellious tribes in the north, particularly the Caledonians. Establishing his base at Eboracum (York), Severus led a series of campaigns that pushed deep into Caledonian territory, aiming to secure Roman control. However, the harsh terrain and fierce resistance hampered lasting success. Severus's health deteriorated, and he died in York in 211 AD. His sons, Caracalla and Geta, succeeded him but soon returned to Rome. Severus's campaigns were part of Rome's broader efforts to secure its northern borders, though they ultimately failed to achieve permanent pacification.

250-270 AD: Economic and Security Challenges

During the mid-3rd century, Roman Britain faced significant economic difficulties and security threats. The province suffered from inflation, devaluation of currency, and disruptions in trade due to increased raids by Picts, Scots, and Saxons. These external pressures, coupled with internal instability, strained the Roman military and administrative structures. Defensive measures included fortifying towns and constructing coastal defenses like the Saxon Shore forts. Despite these efforts, the period marked a decline in prosperity and the beginning of challenges that would ultimately contribute to the weakening of Roman control over Britain.

287 AD: Carausius' Breakaway State

Carausius, a Roman naval commander, declared himself emperor of Britain and northern Gaul in 287 AD after seizing power during a period of military and political instability. He established a breakaway regime, minting his own coins and bolstering the defense against Saxon pirates and Frankish raiders. Carausius leveraged his naval strength to maintain control, creating a de facto independent state. His rule ended in 293 AD when his finance minister, Allectus, assassinated him. Allectus ruled until 296 AD, when Emperor Constantius Chlorus launched an invasion that successfully reintegrated Britain into the Roman Empire, ending the secession.

367-368 AD: The Great Conspiracy

The Great Conspiracy (Barbarica Conspiratio) in 367-368 AD was a coordinated uprising against Roman Britain by Picts, Scots, Saxons, and possibly Roman military mutineers. This multifaceted assault overwhelmed Roman defenses, leading to widespread devastation. The attackers breached Hadrian's Wall and raided deep into the province. The Roman response, led by Count Theodosius (father of the future Emperor Theodosius I), was swift and decisive. He restored order, reformed the administration, and rebuilt fortifications. The Great Conspiracy exposed vulnerabilities in Britain's defenses and underscored the increasing pressure from external threats and internal dissent in the late Roman period.

383 AD: Magnus Maximus

Magnus Maximus, a Roman general stationed in Britain, declared himself emperor in 383 AD and withdrew a significant portion of the Roman army from Britain to support his claim. He established himself as a ruler in Gaul and Spain, challenging the central Roman authority. Maximus's usurpation left Britain with diminished military defenses, increasing its vulnerability to external attacks. His actions contributed to the gradual weakening of Roman control in the province. After being defeated and executed by Emperor Theodosius I in 388 AD, Maximus's departure marked the beginning of the end of effective Roman rule in Britain.

410 AD: End of Roman Rule

The traditional date for the end of Roman rule in Britain is 410 AD, when Emperor Honorius purportedly sent a rescript advising the Britons to look to their own defense. This followed a period of increasing internal strife and external pressures, as Rome could no longer afford to maintain and defend distant provinces. The withdrawal of Roman military and administrative presence left Britain to fend for itself. This led to the fragmentation of authority and the rise of local leaders. The end of Roman rule marked the beginning of the transition to the early medieval period and the eventual Anglo-Saxon settlement.

Mid-5th Century AD: Anglo-Saxon Settlement

Following the Roman withdrawal, Britain saw the gradual arrival and settlement of Anglo-Saxon tribes, including the Angles, Saxons, and Jutes. These groups established their own kingdoms, such as Wessex, Mercia, and Northumbria, gradually replacing Roman institutions and culture. This period, often referred to as the Dark Ages, was characterized by a decline in urban life and literacy. The Anglo-Saxon settlement brought significant cultural and linguistic changes, laying the foundations for the English nation. Archaeological evidence, such as burial sites and artifacts, provides insights into this transformative era, marking the end of Roman Britain and the beginning of medieval England.

Understanding the Romans

What precisely spurred the Roman Empire to extend its formidable reach across the Channel? This question, both simple and profound, invites us to consider not just the overt displays of power or the lure of wealth, but the intricate web of motivations that drove Roman imperial ambitions.

To understand the Roman invasion of Britain is to uncover the layers of economic, military, and political imperatives that propelled one of history's greatest empires to venture into this distant, mist-shrouded isle.

The economic motivations, for instance, cannot be understated. Britain was reputed to be a land rich in resources—minerals like tin and lead, and agricultural wealth that promised to be a bountiful supply for the Roman economy. But to view the invasion merely as a quest for economic gain would be an oversimplification.

The military aspect, the desire for glory, and the strategic need to secure the Empire's northern frontier from the 'barbarian' threats beyond played equally compelling roles in this historical undertaking. Moreover, the political motivations—both within the Roman state and in Britain—added layers of complexity to the invasion narrative.

The allure of conquering Britain held the promise of political prestige for Roman leaders, an opportunity to cement their legacy within the annals of Roman greatness.

Yet, common misconceptions abound. Many have romanticized the Roman invasion as a clash of civilizations, an inevitable confrontation between the civilized world and barbarism. This perspective, while compelling in its narrative simplicity, fails to account for the nuanced interplay of factors that drove the Roman Empire to invade.

It overlooks the pre-existing connections between Britain and the Roman world, the diplomatic exchanges, and the Britons who had already integrated into the Roman economic and cultural spheres before the invasion.

Our approach diverges from traditional narratives by emphasizing the interconnectedness of economic, military, and political motivations, rather than isolating them as independent causes. This holistic perspective allows us to appreciate the complexity of Roman decision-making processes and the multifaceted nature of imperial expansion.

By integrating the analysis of archaeological findings, historical records, and economic data, we offer a more nuanced understanding of why Rome turned its gaze towards Britain.

Consider, for example, the strategic placement of Roman forts and roads following the invasion. These were not merely military installations but part of a larger economic strategy to control trade routes and integrate the British economy into the broader Roman world.

The establishment of Londinium (modern-day London) as a thriving commercial center is a testament to the economic underpinnings of Roman military strategy. Similarly, the promotion of Roman citizenship and the adoption of Roman laws facilitated not just political control but economic integration and cultural assimilation.

Anticipating potential skepticism, some may argue that attributing such strategic foresight to Roman planners overlooks the opportunistic nature of Roman expansion. However, by examining the evidence through the lens of our integrative approach, we can see that Roman actions in Britain were both opportunistic and part of a broader strategic vision.

The Roman Empire was adept at leveraging immediate opportunities within a long-term framework of strategic planning, illustrating a sophisticated understanding of empire-building that went beyond mere conquest.

In applying this perspective to the study of Roman Britain, readers are encouraged to look beyond the surface of historical events. By considering the economic strategies behind military campaigns, the political ambitions underpinning economic actions, and the cultural implications of political decisions, we can gain a deeper understanding of the complex forces that shaped Roman Britain.

This approach not only enriches our comprehension of the past but also offers insights into the dynamics of power, culture, and economy that continue to influence the world today.

Delving deeper into the Roman invasion of Britain, we must scrutinize the precise mechanisms and strategies employed by Roman military tacticians. The Roman military machine was not merely a force of brute strength but a sophisticated entity that utilized a combination of advanced engineering, psychological warfare, and strategic diplomacy to achieve its ends.

The construction of the Roman roads, for instance, serves as a prime example of Rome's strategic acumen. These roads were not built solely for the purpose of facilitating the rapid movement of troops. They also played a crucial role in the economic integration of the British Isles into the Roman economy, enhancing trade routes and ensuring the smooth flow of goods and resources back to the heart of the empire. Moreover, the psychological impact of such infrastructural feats on both the Roman soldiers and the native Britons cannot be overstated. For the former, it was a tangible manifestation of Roman superiority and inevitability of their dominion. For the latter, these roads were a stark symbol of the invaders' power, a daily reminder of their presence, and an indication of the futility of resistance.

The use of Roman forts further illustrates the multifaceted strategy of Roman expansion. Positioned strategically across the landscape, these forts served not only as military bastions but also as administrative centers, facilitating the Romanization of

Britain. They became nuclei of Roman culture, spreading the Latin language, Roman laws, and customs, thereby integrating the local population into the Roman world. This subtle blend of military might and cultural assimilation was pivotal in securing Roman control over Britain.

Furthermore, the Roman approach to local tribes was marked by a nuanced blend of coercion and collaboration. While the Romans did not hesitate to crush dissent and rebellion with overwhelming force, they also employed diplomacy, establishing alliances with certain tribes. These alliances, often sealed with the granting of Roman citizenship to tribal leaders, created a network of client kingdoms. Such a strategy not only reduced the need for direct military intervention but also facilitated the peaceful expansion of Roman influence and culture.

The economic dimension of the Roman invasion, particularly the exploitation of Britain's mineral wealth, was closely intertwined with its military and administrative strategies. The Romans invested in mining operations, extracting significant quantities of lead, silver, and tin. These resources were crucial not just for the Roman economy but also for the empire's military-industrial complex, contributing to the production of weapons, armor, and other military paraphernalia. The strategic development of such economic resources underscores the integrated approach of the Romans to the conquest and control of Britain.

In light of these considerations, the Roman conquest of Britain emerges as a sophisticated campaign that was as much about economic integration, cultural assimilation, and political maneuvering as it was about military conquest. The genius of

Roman strategy lay in its ability to adapt and evolve, to blend force with diplomacy, and to integrate conquered peoples into the Roman world, thereby ensuring the long-term stability and prosperity of the empire's provinces.

As we peel away the layers of Roman military strategy, we uncover a complex picture of conquest that challenges simplistic narratives of domination. The Roman invasion of Britain was a multifaceted endeavor, characterized by strategic foresight, economic savvy, and a profound understanding of human psychology. It is a testament to the Roman Empire's ability to project power far beyond its borders, not just through the force of arms but through the subtler instruments of culture, economy, and governance.

Transitioning from the strategies and mechanisms of the Roman invasion, our narrative arc bends towards the uprising led by Boudicca in 60 AD, a seminal event that highlights the complexities and challenges of Roman rule in Britain. This pivotal moment in the history of Roman Britain not only underscores the resistance of the native population but also serves as a lens through which we can examine the broader implications of Roman imperialism.

Boudicca, queen of the Iceni tribe, emerges as a central figure in this narrative, embodying the fierce spirit of resistance against Roman oppression. Her story, rooted in tragedy and defiance, begins with the Roman decision to annex the kingdom of the Iceni, a stark violation of the agreements made with her late husband, King Prasutagus. The subsequent mistreatment of Boudicca and her daughters by Roman officials ignited a flame of rebellion that would sweep across the eastern provinces of Roman Britain.

The primary issue at the heart of Boudicca's uprising was not only the personal grievance of a bereaved queen but a more profound challenge to the legitimacy and sustainability of Roman rule. The significance of this challenge lies in its ability to galvanize a broad coalition of tribes, transcending traditional rivalries and uniting them in a common cause against a common enemy. This uprising, therefore, serves as a poignant reminder of the tensions that simmered beneath the surface of Roman Britain, threatening the stability of its dominion.

The methods employed by Boudicca and her allies in confronting the Roman forces were characterized by a combination of guerrilla tactics and direct engagements. They leveraged their intimate knowledge of the terrain, launching surprise attacks and ambushing Roman detachments. The sacking of Camulodunum (modern-day Colchester), Londinium (London), and Verulamium (St. Albans) were not only military objectives but also symbolic acts of defiance, aimed at dismantling the symbols of Roman authority and culture.

The outcomes of Boudicca's rebellion, while ultimately culminating in the defeat of the Briton forces, had far-reaching implications. The rebellion resulted in the destruction of significant Roman settlements and a heavy toll on the Roman military presence in Britain. It prompted a reassessment of Roman administrative and military strategies, leading to a more conciliatory approach towards the native tribes. The Roman response to the uprising, under the leadership of Governor Suetonius Paulinus, exemplifies the adaptive strategies of the empire, emphasizing the blend of military reprisal and diplomatic engagement to restore stability.

What can be learned from Boudicca's uprising is manifold. It illustrates the precarious nature of colonial rule and the potential for indigenous resistance to coalesce around charismatic leadership. The uprising challenges the notion of Roman invincibility and underscores the importance of strategic flexibility and cultural sensitivity in governance. Furthermore, it highlights the role of individual agency in the midst of historical forces, with Boudicca's leadership serving as a catalyst for one of the most significant challenges to Roman authority in Britain.

By situating Boudicca's uprising within the broader context of Roman Britain, we gain insight into the dynamic interplay between conqueror and conquered. This case study not only enriches our understanding of a critical juncture in Roman Britain but also invites us to reflect on the enduring themes of resistance, identity, and the struggle for autonomy. Through the lens of this rebellion, we are able to glimpse the complexities of empire, the nuances of colonial relationships, and the indomitable spirit of those who resist domination.

In the wake of Boudicca's rebellion, a comparative analysis of Roman military tactics and technology with those of the Celtic tribes of Britain comes into sharp relief. This juxtaposition not only illuminates the divergent approaches to warfare but also offers insights into the broader socio-political and cultural implications of these differences.

The Roman military machine, renowned for its discipline, organization, and technological innovation, stood in stark contrast to the more loosely organized, tribal warfare of the Britons. The Roman legions, with their rigorous training regimens, standardized equipment, and complex battlefield formations, such as the testudo shield wall formation commonly seen in modern portrayals of Roman warfare, exemplified a highly efficient, professional fighting force. This was complemented by Roman military engineering prowess, evident in the construction of fortifications, siege engines, and the aforementioned roads, which facilitated not only rapid troop movements but also strategic control over key territories.

Conversely, the Celtic tribes of Britain, though fierce and valiant warriors, relied more on individual bravery and the element of surprise than on disciplined formations or advanced technology. Their tactics often involved swift, raid-like strikes and ambushes, taking advantage of the densely wooded landscapes of Britain to launch surprise attacks against Roman forces. The chariot, a hallmark of Celtic warfare, exemplified this approach, allowing for rapid, mobile assaults that could harry and disorient a more heavily armed and armored foe.

The differences in weaponry and armor between the two also reflected their contrasting military philosophies. Roman soldiers were equipped with the gladius, a short, double-edged sword designed for close combat, and the pilum, a heavy javelin that could penetrate enemy shields. Their armor, including the lorica segmentata, offered substantial protection against the slashing and stabbing attacks typical of Celtic combat. The Britons, on the other hand, favored longer swords and spears, and while their warriors often went into battle with little to no armor, they relied on mobility and ferocity to overwhelm their adversaries.

These divergent military approaches had profound implications for the nature of Roman and Celtic encounters. Roman tactics and technology, designed for open-field battles and sieges, were initially less effective in the guerrilla-style warfare practiced by the Britons. However, the adaptability and resourcefulness of Roman commanders eventually allowed for the development of counter-strategies that mitigated the advantages of Celtic warfare tactics.

Moreover, the contrast between Roman and Celtic warfare extends beyond the battlefield, reflecting broader cultural and societal differences. The Roman emphasis on discipline, hierarchy, and the integration of military technology into a broader strategic framework speaks to a civilization deeply invested in the concepts of order, control, and expansion. The Celtic approach, with its emphasis on individual valor, tribal loyalty, and a more organic relationship with the landscape, reflects a society for whom warfare was not just a means of territorial conquest but also a crucial component of social identity and cohesion.

This exploration of Roman and Celtic military tactics and technology, therefore, not only sheds light on the specific dynamics of conquest and resistance but also contributes to our understanding of the complex processes of cultural interaction and integration that define human history.

Having delineated the stark contrasts between Roman and Celtic military strategies and their broader cultural implications, our narrative now shifts towards the administrative machinations that underpinned Roman rule in Britain.

This shift from the battlefield to the realm of governance and civil administration reveals another layer of Roman strategy, pivotal to the empire's long-term objectives in Britain.

The establishment and maintenance of Roman administrative structures were not merely ancillary to military conquest but were central to the process of Romanization and the effective control of the province.

The Roman administrative apparatus in Britain was characterized by a complex hierarchy of officials and a sophisticated legal system, designed to integrate the province into the broader imperial framework.

At the pinnacle of this system was the Roman governor, appointed by the emperor, who wielded both military and civil authority.

The governor was supported by a retinue of legates, procurators, and other officials, responsible for various aspects of administration, including finance, justice, and the oversight of public works.

One of the most significant administrative initiatives undertaken by the Romans was the establishment of municipia and coloniae - settlements with distinct legal statuses, which served as beacons of Roman culture and governance.

These settlements were strategically located, often near former tribal centers, and played a crucial role in the dissemination of Roman laws, customs, and language.

The inhabitants of these settlements, including veterans of the Roman army and local elites who had aligned themselves with Roman rule, became the vanguard of the Romanization process, facilitating the integration of the broader population into the Roman socio-political and economic system.

The legal framework introduced by the Romans, grounded in Roman law, was another instrument of administrative control and cultural integration.

This legal system, with its emphasis on written statutes, public trials, and the rights of citizens, represented a significant departure from the tribal legal traditions that had previously prevailed in Britain.

The introduction of Roman law not only facilitated the administration of justice but also served as a vehicle for the spread of Roman values and norms.

Furthermore, the Roman approach to infrastructure development was integral to their administrative strategy.

The construction of roads, aqueducts, and public buildings was not only about improving the efficiency of military and economic logistics but also about manifesting the power and sophistication of Roman civilization.

These infrastructure projects, often undertaken by the Roman army, employed a significant number of local laborers, thereby creating a direct economic linkage between the Roman occupiers and the native population.

This not only contributed to the economic prosperity of the province but also engendered a sense of shared interests and interdependence between Romans and Britons.

However, the Roman administrative system in Britain was not without its challenges.

Issues of taxation, land ownership, and local governance often led to tensions and, in some cases, outright resistance.

The Roman response to these challenges was typically pragmatic, involving a combination of negotiation, adaptation of existing practices, and, when necessary, force.

The ability of the Roman administration to navigate these complex issues was testament to its flexibility and the empire's overarching strategic goal of creating a stable, integrated province that would contribute to the wealth and security of the Roman world.

In examining the administrative underpinnings of Roman rule in Britain, we gain insight into the empire's broader strategies for governance and integration.

The meticulous organization of the province, the strategic deployment of legal and economic tools, and the pragmatic approach to local challenges highlight the Romans' sophisticated understanding of empire-building.

This administrative strategy, in concert with military conquest and cultural assimilation, forged a province that, despite its geographical remoteness and initial resistance, became an integral part of the Roman Empire, contributing to its prosperity and stability.

With the administrative framework of Roman Britain firmly established, our attention shifts towards the economic transformation that ensued under Roman rule. This aspect of Roman influence, perhaps more than any other, had a profound and lasting impact on the economic landscape of Britain, marking a departure from the pre-Roman economy that was predominantly agrarian and tribal-based, towards a more diversified and market-oriented economy.

The introduction of Roman economic practices and structures facilitated a significant increase in agricultural productivity. The Romans introduced new crops, improved farming techniques, and better livestock breeding practices, which collectively contributed to a surplus in agricultural production. This surplus not only supported the local population but also supplied the Roman army and was traded across the empire, integrating Britain into a vast network of trade and commerce.

Moreover, the Roman occupation heralded the beginning of industrial activities in Britain on a scale previously unseen. The exploitation of mineral resources, particularly in Wales and the Pennines, was accelerated under Roman guidance. The extraction of lead, silver, and tin became highly organized, with the Romans introducing advanced mining techniques and technologies. These resources were crucial for the Roman economy, serving not only as materials for coinage and luxury items but also for practical uses in plumbing, construction, and military equipment. The establishment of such industries created a ripple effect, stimulating the development of secondary industries, trade, and urbanization.

The role of Roman cities in transforming the British economy cannot be overstated. Cities such as Londinium (London), Eboracum (York), and Aquae Sulis (Bath) became centers of trade, manufacturing, and cultural exchange. These urban centers attracted merchants, artisans, and entrepreneurs from across the Roman Empire, facilitating the exchange of goods, ideas, and technologies. The urban economy was characterized by a high degree of specialization, with different regions and towns developing niches based on local resources and expertise.

Another significant aspect of the Roman economic transformation was the introduction of a sophisticated monetary system. The use of coinage became widespread, facilitating trade and commerce. This monetary economy helped to standardize economic transactions, reduce transaction costs, and integrate the British economy into the broader Roman monetary system. The impact of this shift towards a monetized economy was far-reaching, influencing social structures, wealth distribution, and economic strategies.

The Roman taxation system also played a pivotal role in the economic transformation of Britain. Taxes were levied on land, goods, and individuals, creating a steady revenue stream for the Roman state. While taxation was a source of resentment and, at times, conflict, it also contributed to the administrative and military stability of the province, enabling further economic development. The Roman tax system, in conjunction with military spending and infrastructure development, acted as a form of fiscal stimulus, promoting economic activity and growth.

However, the economic advancements introduced by the Romans were not uniformly beneficial across all strata of British society. The integration of Britain into the Roman economy led to significant social and economic disparities. The Romanization of the elite, who often benefited disproportionately from the new economic opportunities, widened the gap between the wealthy and the poor. Additionally, the dependence on the Roman market and the shift towards a specialized, export-oriented economy made Britain vulnerable to fluctuations in the Roman economy.

In analyzing the economic transformation of Roman Britain, it becomes evident that the Roman occupation was a catalyst for profound economic changes. These changes, driven by the integration of Britain into the Roman world, had lasting impacts on the economic structures, social hierarchies, and urbanization patterns of Britain. The legacy of Roman economic policies and practices continued to influence the development of Britain long after the decline of Roman power, laying the foundation for the economic landscape of medieval and modern Britain.

Daily Life Under Roman Rule

With the economic transformation of Roman Britain thoroughly explored, our narrative now ventures into the intricate web of social dynamics and cultural integration that marked this period of history. It is within this social crucible that the most profound impacts of Roman rule can be discerned—impacts that reshaped the identity and fabric of British society.

The imposition of Roman culture, governance, and economic systems upon the Celtic tribes of Britain set the stage for a complex process of cultural assimilation and resistance. This process was not uniform or unidirectional; rather, it was characterized by a dynamic interplay between Roman and native elements, giving rise to a unique cultural synthesis that would define Roman Britain.

One of the most visible signs of this cultural integration was the adoption of Roman lifestyles among the British elite. Influenced by the prestige and perceived sophistication of Roman customs, many of Britain's tribal leaders began to adopt Roman dress, language, and dining practices. This adoption was not merely superficial but indicative of a deeper shift in values and identity among the elite, who sought to align themselves with the power and status of the Roman Empire.

However, the process of Romanization was not limited to the elite. The spread of Roman urban centers across Britain facilitated the broader dissemination of Roman culture. Public baths, amphitheaters, and temples became focal points of urban life, introducing the local population to Roman architectural styles, religious practices, and entertainment. These urban centers acted as crucibles of cultural exchange, where Roman and Celtic traditions could interact and influence one another.

The Roman religious landscape in Britain further exemplifies the complex nature of cultural integration. While the Romans introduced the worship of their pantheon of gods, they also showed a remarkable degree of syncretism, adopting and integrating Celtic deities into their religious practices. This syncretism was not merely a top-down imposition but reflected genuine engagement and exchange between Roman and Celtic spiritual traditions. Such interactions suggest a level of mutual respect and accommodation that challenges simplistic narratives of cultural domination.

Education and literacy represent another dimension of Roman influence on British society. The introduction of Latin as the language of administration, law, and trade significantly impacted literacy and education. For the native Britons, proficiency in Latin became a valuable skill, opening up opportunities for advancement within the Roman administrative and economic systems. This linguistic shift also facilitated the spread of Roman legal and philosophical ideas, contributing to the intellectual enrichment of British society.

Despite these profound influences, it is crucial to recognize that the process of cultural integration was not seamless or uniformly accepted. Resistance to Romanization persisted, particularly in rural areas and among the lower strata of society, where attachment to Celtic traditions remained strong. This resistance underscores the diversity of experiences and attitudes towards Roman rule within Britain, highlighting the resilience of local identities and practices.

In examining the social and cultural dynamics of Roman Britain, we uncover a narrative of complexity and contradiction. The Roman occupation initiated a period of profound change, driving the integration of disparate cultures and the emergence of a new social order. Yet, within this process of transformation, there was also continuity, as the enduring elements of Celtic culture persisted and adapted to the new Roman reality. This duality, characterized by both change and continuity, defines the legacy of Roman Britain, illustrating the enduring power of cultural exchange and adaptation in shaping human societies.

As we delve further into Roman Britain, it becomes increasingly apparent that the culinary realm serves as a microcosm of the broader processes of cultural integration and adaptation.

The introduction of Roman dietary practices and foodstuffs into Britain not only transformed the culinary landscape but also offers a fascinating lens through which to explore the intersections of culture, power, and identity.

The Roman diet, characterized by its diversity and sophistication, was a reflection of an empire that had assimilated culinary traditions from across its vast territories.

The incorporation of new foodstuffs such as wine, olive oil, and a variety of fruits and vegetables, into the British diet, marked a significant departure from the indigenous fare.

These items, along with the Roman penchant for sauces and spices, introduced Britons to a palette of flavors previously unknown.

However, the Roman culinary influence extended beyond mere ingredients.

The Roman approach to dining—a social and often elaborate affair—introduced new customs and etiquette to the British table.

The triclinium, or dining room, became a symbol of Roman sophistication, a place where the elite could display their wealth, status, and adherence to Roman culture through the ritual of the convivium, or banquet.

This adoption of Roman dining practices by the British elite was not merely an emulation of foreign customs but served as a means of social distinction and cultural alignment with the empire's ruling class.

Yet, the culinary integration was not one-sided.

The Romans, in their pragmatic approach to governance and assimilation, also incorporated elements of Celtic cuisine into their diet.

The cultivation of local crops and the consumption of native game and seafood reflected a degree of culinary syncretism, a blending of Roman and British tastes that mirrored the larger process of cultural integration.

The economic implications of these dietary changes were profound.

The demand for imported goods such as wine and olive oil spurred the development of trade networks, connecting Britain more closely to the continental economy.

Meanwhile, the Roman influence on agriculture—through the introduction of new crops and farming techniques—boosted local production, contributing to the economic prosperity and transformation of the province.

Moreover, the archaeological evidence of Roman kitchens, utensils, and dining ware in Britain provides tangible proof of the Romanization of domestic life.

These artifacts, ranging from sophisticated glassware and pottery to simple cooking implements, tell a story of adaptation and change.

They reveal how ordinary Britons, not just the elite, were touched by Roman culinary practices, integrating these foreign elements into their daily lives.

In analyzing the culinary transformation of Roman Britain, we observe not just a change in diet but a profound shift in social practices, economic relationships, and cultural identity.

The Roman table, with its exotic foods and elaborate rituals, became a site of cultural negotiation, where power was exercised, identities were shaped, and the boundaries between Roman and Briton were both reinforced and blurred.

This exploration of Roman culinary influence in Britain thus provides a richly textured understanding of the complex dynamics of empire and assimilation.

It highlights the role of everyday practices in the processes of cultural change and underscores the significance of food as a vector of social and cultural integration.

Through the lens of cuisine, we gain insight into the subtleties of Roman power and the resilience of British identity, illuminating the intricate ways in which cultures merge, adapt, and persist.

As we delve into the intricate interplay between Roman and Celtic spiritual practices, a nuanced understanding of religious syncretism in Roman Britain emerges. This phenomenon, wherein the religious beliefs and practices of the Roman conquerors and the Celtic inhabitants intertwined, offers profound insights into the broader processes of cultural interaction and assimilation that characterized this epoch.

The Romans, known for their pragmatic approach to religion, were adept at incorporating the deities and religious practices of conquered peoples into their own pantheon. This inclusive approach encouraged the facilitation and acceptance of Roman rule among subject populations.

The worship of Sulis Minerva at the temple in Aquae Sulis (modern-day Bath) stands as a quintessential example of this syncretism. Sulis, a local goddess associated with the healing waters of the spring, was equated with Minerva, the Roman goddess of wisdom and strategy. The resulting amalgam, Sulis Minerva, embodied the fusion of local and Roman religious identities, serving both as a symbol of Roman authority and a concession to local religious traditions. This coalescence of deities not only eased the transition to Roman rule but also allowed for the continuation of indigenous religious practices under a Roman guise.

Moreover, the introduction of the cult of the Emperor in Britain further illustrates the complexities of religious life in Roman Britain. The cult, which mandated the worship of the Roman Emperor as a god, was a tool of political and religious integration, linking the stability of the Empire with the divine favor bestowed upon the Emperor. While this practice was met with acceptance in many parts of the Roman world, its reception in Britain was mixed, reflecting the varying degrees of Romanization among the population. In regions where Roman influence was strong, the cult reinforced loyalty to the Empire; in less Romanized areas, it was often blended with existing Celtic practices, resulting in a distinctive local variant of Emperor worship.

The archaeological record provides further evidence of religious syncretism through the discovery of votive offerings and inscriptions dedicated to both Roman and Celtic deities, sometimes within the same sacred space. These findings indicate a level of religious tolerance and flexibility that facilitated the coexistence of multiple religious traditions within Roman Britain. Such practices not only underscore the adaptability of Roman religion but also highlight the resilience of Celtic religious identity, as indigenous beliefs were not eradicated but rather recontextualized within the Roman religious framework.

This exploration of religious syncretism in Roman Britain sheds light on the complex dynamics of cultural exchange and adaptation. It reveals how religion served as a conduit for Romanization, while simultaneously providing a space for the preservation and transformation of Celtic spiritual traditions. The interweaving of Roman and Celtic religions reflects the broader theme of syncretism that characterizes Roman Britain, where the interaction of diverse cultures gave rise to a unique hybrid identity that was neither wholly Roman nor entirely Celtic.

By examining the religious landscape of Roman Britain, we gain deeper insights into the mechanisms of cultural integration and the multifaceted nature of identity in the ancient world. This analysis not only enriches our understanding of Roman Britain but also contributes to the broader discourse on the role of religion in the processes of cultural contact and change.

In the sphere of education and intellectual life, the Roman occupation of Britain instigated significant shifts, further illuminating the multifaceted nature of cultural integration.

The Romans, with their sophisticated system of education, introduced formal schooling and the study of Latin literature, philosophy, and law to the British Isles. This educational revolution not only facilitated the Romanization of the British elite but also served as a vehicle for the broader dissemination of Roman cultural values and intellectual traditions.

The establishment of schools in major urban centers such as Londinium and Eboracum provided the sons of the British elite with access to a Roman education, equipping them with the skills necessary to participate in the administrative and economic life of the empire.

The curriculum, centered on the trivium (grammar, rhetoric, and logic) and the quadrivium (arithmetic, geometry, music, and astronomy), reflected the Roman ideal of a well-rounded education, aimed at cultivating the intellect and preparing individuals for public service.

Moreover, the Roman emphasis on legal education had a profound impact on the development of British legal institutions. The study of Roman law introduced concepts of justice and governance that were distinct from the tribal customs that had previously prevailed.

This infusion of Roman legal principles contributed to the evolution of a more structured and unified legal system in Britain, one that would endure well beyond the Roman period.

However, the Roman approach to education was not without its critics. Some members of the British population viewed the adoption of Roman educational practices as a threat to their cultural heritage and identity.

This tension highlights the complexity of cultural assimilation, where the integration of new ideas and practices can lead to both enrichment and resistance.

The intellectual life of Roman Britain was also enriched by the presence of libraries and the circulation of texts, both Roman and Greek.

These repositories of knowledge served as centers of intellectual exchange, where ideas could be discussed and debated.

The presence of such institutions indicates a vibrant intellectual culture that transcended the practical concerns of administration and commerce, fostering a climate of inquiry and debate that was characteristic of the Roman world.

Furthermore, the archaeological evidence of writing tablets, inscriptions, and manuscripts in Britain attests to the spread of literacy and the importance of written communication in Roman society.

The ability to read and write in Latin was not only a marker of social status but also a practical skill that facilitated the integration of Britons into the Roman administrative system.

This widespread literacy had a democratizing effect, allowing for greater participation in the civic life of the province and the empire at large.

The impact of Roman education and intellectual traditions on Britain was multifaceted, contributing to the Romanization of the elite while also sowing the seeds of resistance among those who viewed these changes as a dilution of their cultural identity.

This dynamic interplay between acceptance and resistance underscores the complexity of cultural integration in Roman Britain, where the forces of change encountered the resilience of tradition.

As we contemplate the legacy of Roman education in Britain, we are reminded of the enduring power of ideas and the role of education in shaping societies.

The transmission of Roman intellectual traditions to Britain not only transformed the educational landscape but also left an indelible mark on British culture, influencing the development of legal, philosophical, and scientific thought in the centuries that followed.

The exploration of education and intellectual life in Roman Britain thus adds another layer to our understanding of the processes of cultural integration and identity formation.

It reveals how the Roman occupation served as a catalyst for intellectual and educational advancements, which, in turn, played a critical role in the shaping of British society.

Through the lens of education, we gain deeper insights into the complexities of Roman Britain, a society characterized by both the adoption of Roman ways and the preservation of indigenous traditions.

Emerging from the intellectual arenas of Roman Britain, we now turn our gaze to the realm of entertainment, a facet of Roman culture that wielded substantial influence over the social fabric of the province.

The Romans, renowned for their appreciation of leisure and spectacle, introduced a variety of entertainments that became integral to public life and communal identity in Britain.

The construction of amphitheaters in key urban centers such as Londinium, Camulodunum, and Verulamium marked a significant shift in the landscape of British entertainment.

These grand structures, often capable of accommodating thousands of spectators, hosted a wide array of events, from gladiatorial combat to theatrical performances.

The amphitheater, as a space of mass entertainment, served not merely as a venue for spectacle but also as a crucible for the Romanization of British society.

Gladiatorial games, perhaps the most iconic of Roman entertainments, exemplified the complex interplay between spectacle, violence, and social order.

These contests, which pitted combatants against each other or against wild beasts, were not mere bloodsports but ritualized expressions of power and dominion.

For the Roman authorities in Britain, the games served as a tool of social control, demonstrating the might of the Empire and the futility of resistance.

Yet, for the common people, they provided a form of escapism and a spectacle in which the themes of life, death, and honor were dramatically enacted.

The public baths, another import from the Roman world, played a pivotal role in the social and cultural life of Roman Britain.

Far more than mere facilities for hygiene, these baths functioned as centers of community life, where individuals from various strata of society could gather, converse, and engage in leisure activities.

The baths embodied the Roman ideal of otium (leisure), blending relaxation with social interaction and intellectual discourse.

In the steam-filled rooms of the baths, the cultural and social boundaries of Roman Britain were both reinforced and negotiated, as the communal aspect of bathing facilitated a unique form of social integration.

Theatrical performances, though less documented than other forms of Roman entertainment, were undoubtedly a part of the cultural landscape of Roman Britain.

Drawing on a rich tradition of Roman and Greek drama, these performances likely ranged from high tragedy to farcical comedy, reflecting the complexities of human experience.

The theater, like the amphitheater, served as a space where Roman cultural narratives were enacted and absorbed, contributing to the shaping of collective identities and values.

Through the lens of entertainment, we observe not only the Romanization of British society but also the resilience of indigenous traditions.

The adoption of Roman forms of entertainment did not result in the wholesale erasure of local customs and practices.

Instead, a process of adaptation and synthesis occurred, where Roman and Celtic elements merged to create a distinctive cultural milieu.

This dynamic interplay between adoption and adaptation highlights the fluidity of cultural boundaries and the capacity of societies to integrate and transform external influences.

The exploration of Roman entertainment in Britain thus offers valuable insights into the mechanisms of cultural exchange and integration.

It reveals how entertainment functioned as a medium of Romanization, serving both to propagate Roman cultural norms and to create spaces for the negotiation of identity and belonging.

In the amphitheaters, baths, and theaters of Roman Britain, we find a society engaged in an ongoing dialogue with itself, continually reshaping its cultural landscape in response to the challenges and opportunities of Roman rule.

As we delve further into the cultural exchange that flourished under Roman rule, it becomes increasingly clear that language played a pivotal role in the transformation of society in Roman Britain. The Latin language, a cornerstone of Roman culture and administration, emerged as a powerful tool of integration, facilitating communication across the diverse communities within the province.

The spread of Latin went beyond mere practicality; it symbolized the Romanization of the British Isles, embedding itself within the fabric of daily life, commerce, and governance.

The adoption of Latin by the British populace was neither uniform nor uncontested. Among the elite, fluency in Latin was a marker of status and allegiance to the Roman state, enabling their participation in the administrative and legal systems imposed by Rome.

For the common people, however, the penetration of Latin into everyday language was gradual, often coexisting with native Celtic languages in a bilingual landscape. This linguistic duality served as a testament to the complex identity of Roman Britain, where Roman and Celtic influences intermingled and coexisted.

The impact of Latin on the local languages was profound, influencing vocabulary, syntax, and even the development of writing systems. The introduction of the Roman alphabet facilitated the transition from oral to written culture, allowing for the documentation of history, transactions, and legal proceedings.

This shift not only enhanced communication and record-keeping but also contributed to the cultural and intellectual legacy of Britain, preserving knowledge that would otherwise have been lost to time.

Yet, the spread of Latin also had its detractors. For some, the imposition of the Latin language represented a loss of cultural heritage, an erasure of Celtic identity in favor of Roman norms and values.

Resistance to Romanization, therefore, was not only a matter of armed rebellion or political dissent but also manifested in the preservation of Celtic languages and traditions.

This resistance underscores the resilience of local cultures facing the overwhelming influence of a global empire.

The role of language in Roman Britain highlights the nuanced dynamics of power, identity, and resistance that characterized the province. The Latin language, as a vehicle of Roman culture, played a crucial role in the processes of integration and Romanization.

Yet, the persistence of Celtic languages and traditions amidst Roman dominance reflects the strength of local identities and the limits of cultural assimilation.

In exploring the linguistic landscape of Roman Britain, we uncover another layer of its complex history, one that illustrates the enduring impact of language on culture, society, and identity.

The legacy of Latin in Britain, with its contributions to the development of the English language, legal systems, and literary traditions, is a testament to the transformative power of language.

At the same time, the survival and revival of Celtic languages in certain regions of Britain remind us of the capacity of cultures to resist and adapt to external influences.

Through the prism of language, Roman Britain emerges as a microcosm of cultural exchange and adaptation, where the forces of Romanization and the resilience of indigenous traditions vied for dominance.

This interplay between assimilation and resistance, between the global and the local, defines the historical narrative of Roman Britain, offering insights into the complexities of cultural integration in the ancient world.

Art, Craftsmanship and Society

As we navigate through the landscape that defined Roman Britain, our attention is inevitably drawn to the realm of art and craftsmanship, a domain where the dialogue between Roman innovation and Celtic tradition unfolds with striking vividness.

The fusion of Roman artistic sensibilities with indigenous British craftsmanship resulted in a distinctive visual culture that bore witness to the complex process of cultural synthesis and adaptation.

Roman influence introduced new materials, techniques, and motifs to the artistic repertoire of Britain, revolutionizing the aesthetics of local craftsmanship.

The introduction of fine pottery, glassware, and metalwork, characterized by intricate designs and superior quality, marked a significant departure from the more utilitarian objects that typified Celtic art.

These Roman imports were not only symbols of prestige and wealth but also served as mediums through which Roman cultural values and tastes were disseminated.

However, the story of art in Roman Britain is not one of mere imposition or assimilation.

The native artisans and craftsmen, while adopting Roman techniques and motifs, infused their works with distinctly Celtic elements, creating hybrid forms that defied simple categorization.

The intricate knotwork and spirals that adorned Celtic art found new expression in Roman Britain, embellished upon stone, metal, and pottery.

This blending of styles speaks to a dialogue between cultures, where the aesthetic sensibilities of the conquerors and the conquered intermingled and enriched one another.

The architectural landscape of Roman Britain further illustrates this synthesis of Roman and Celtic artistry.

The construction of villas, public baths, and temples, in adherence to Roman architectural principles, introduced the British Isles to the grandeur of Roman design.

Yet, these structures often incorporated local materials and techniques, reflecting a pragmatic adaptation to the indigenous environment and resources.

The enduring presence of these edifices, with their Roman foundations and Celtic nuances, serves as a testament to the enduring legacy of cultural exchange.

Moreover, the presence of funerary monuments and inscriptions in Roman Britain provides invaluable insights into the personal identities and social dynamics of the time.

These monuments, often featuring bilingual inscriptions, underscore the coexistence of Roman and Celtic languages and reveal the complex identities of the provincial inhabitants.

They symbolize the intersection of personal and cultural narratives, where individual lives were inscribed within the broader Roman imperial history.

The exploration of art and craftsmanship in Roman Britain thus uncovers a rich cultural interaction, where the forces of Romanization met with the resilience and creativity of Celtic traditions.

This dynamic interplay not only gave rise to a unique visual culture but also contributed to the formation of a distinct provincial identity that navigated the complexities of empire and tradition.

Through the lens of art, Roman Britain emerges as a vibrant arena of cultural synthesis, where the legacy of Rome and the spirit of Britain were woven together in a lasting testament to the power of cultural exchange and adaptation.

Casting our gaze to the Roman architectural footprint in Britain, characterized by grand public buildings, fortifications, and villas, we see it showcased the engineering prowess of the empire but also functioned as visible markers of Roman civilization and order amidst the British landscape.

The construction of public baths, forums, and temples in urban centers across Britain was emblematic of the Roman architectural ethos, which prioritized symmetry, functionality, and a deep reverence for the gods.

These structures, often built on an imposing scale, were designed to inspire awe and allegiance to Rome, serving both practical and ideological purposes.

The public baths, with their sophisticated heating and plumbing systems, exemplified the Roman commitment to hygiene, leisure, and social cohesion, offering a communal space where citizens could engage in the rituals of bathing, exercise, and conversation.

Similarly, the forum, the heart of Roman urban life, functioned as a bustling marketplace and administrative hub, facilitating economic transactions and civic administration.

The presence of temples within these urban complexes underscored the integral role of religion in Roman society, serving as a constant reminder of the pax deorum, the peace of the gods, which underpinned Roman prosperity and power.

The construction of fortifications, such as Hadrian's Wall, further illustrates the strategic application of Roman architecture.

These imposing structures were not merely defensive barriers but symbols of Roman might and the limits of the civilized world.

Positioned at the frontier of the empire, Hadrian's Wall embodied the Roman desire for order and control, demarcating the boundary between the Romanized south and the unconquered north.

Roman villas in Britain, often sprawling estates that combined luxurious living spaces with agricultural production, reflected the Romanization of the British elite.

These villas, with their elaborate mosaics, gardens, and bathhouses, were centers of economic activity and cultural assimilation, where the British aristocracy adopted Roman customs, language, and lifestyles.

The architectural sophistication of these estates, along with their role in promoting agricultural innovation, played a pivotal role in the economic and social transformation of Roman Britain.

Yet, the Roman architectural legacy in Britain was not solely the domain of the elite or the military.

The construction of roads, bridges, and aqueducts transformed the British landscape, facilitating trade, military movements, and communication across the province.

These infrastructural projects, undertaken with remarkable engineering skill, exemplified the Roman commitment to connectivity and integration, knitting the far-flung corners of Britain into the fabric of the empire.

The legacy of Roman architecture in Britain, therefore, extends beyond the physical remnants of buildings and fortifications.

It encompasses a profound transformation of the British landscape and society, where Roman and Celtic elements merged to create a distinctive cultural and spatial environment.

Through the lens of architecture, we witness the Roman Empire's strategy of cultural integration and control, a testament to its ability to shape the societies it conquered.

In examining the architectural and artistic contributions of Rome to Britain, we not only appreciate the aesthetic and structural achievements but also recognize these endeavors as integral components of the Roman imperial project.

The edifices of Roman Britain stand as enduring symbols of the empire's ambition to civilize, control, and integrate, reflecting the complex dynamics of power, identity, and resistance that characterized this period of history.

If we wish to continue to examine the change in society that Rome brought, then the evolution of personal adornment and fashion under Roman influence offers a compelling window into the social transformations that unfolded within this province of the Roman Empire.

The introduction of Roman styles of dress and personal adornment to Britain was not merely an aesthetic imposition but represented a deeper shift in social identities and hierarchies. Roman clothing, characterized by the toga for men and the stola for women, symbolized Roman citizenship and conveyed a sense of civic dignity and belonging.

For the British elite, the adoption of Roman attire was both a marker of allegiance to the Roman state and a means to distinguish themselves from the broader population.

This sartorial assimilation was facilitated by the Romanization of the textile industry in Britain. The establishment of weaving workshops and the introduction of new fibers and dyes expanded the range of textiles available, enhancing the quality and variety of garments.

This transformation was not confined to the elite; it permeated various strata of society, with Roman styles gradually influencing local dress.

Jewelry and personal ornaments, too, reflected the cultural exchanges of Roman Britain. The use of Roman motifs in jewelry design, such as the use of the eagle, the symbol of Jupiter, and other deities, illustrated the amalgamation of Roman and Celtic artistic traditions.

These items served not only as personal adornments but also as symbols of social status and cultural affiliation.

The Roman military also played a pivotal role in the dissemination of fashion and adornment. Soldiers, often hailing from diverse regions of the empire, brought with them their own styles and preferences, contributing to the eclectic mix of influences that characterized Roman Britain's sartorial landscape.

The presence of foreign traders and artisans, attracted by the economic opportunities of the province, further enriched this cultural tapestry.

However, the Roman influence on fashion and adornment in Britain was not universally embraced. Among the rural and lower-class populations, traditional Celtic styles and ornaments persisted, serving as a symbol of resistance to Romanization and a statement of cultural identity.

This dichotomy in dress and adornment underscores the complex interplay of acceptance and resistance that defined Roman Britain, reflecting the broader processes of cultural integration and identity formation.

Rome's Caledonian Challenge

The intricate dance between the Roman Empire and the indigenous populations of Britain, were mediated by the architectural and strategic marvel that is Hadrian's Wall, a fortification that we shall look at more in the next chapter.

The Caledonian tribes, often perceived through the lens of Roman sources as fierce and indomitable warriors, presented a formidable challenge to the Roman ambition of conquering the entirety of Britain.

It was not merely their physical prowess on the battlefield that earned them this reputation, but their strategic use of the rugged Scottish landscape to their advantage, a testament to their deep understanding of guerilla warfare tactics.

This warfare strategy was characterized by swift, unexpected strikes against Roman forces, exploiting the element of surprise and the challenging terrain to offset the numerical and technological superiority of the Roman legions.

The Roman response to this unconventional warfare was a mix of admiration, frustration, and adaptation.

Initially caught off guard by the hit-and-run tactics of the Caledonian tribes, the Roman military machine was forced to rethink its approach to warfare in the northern reaches of Britain.

The construction of Hadrian's Wall, and later the Antonine Wall, can be seen as physical manifestations of this strategic recalibration.

These fortifications were not only defensive structures but also served as bases from which the Romans could launch patrols and counter-insurgency operations, attempting to control and pacify the region.

One of the most notable clashes, the Battle of Mons Graupiusin 83 AD, purportedly saw a large Roman force under the command of General Agricola face off against a significant assembly of Caledonian warriors.

While Roman accounts claim a decisive victory, the lack of a conclusive subjugation of the Caledonian tribes in the aftermath suggests a more complex outcome.

This battle, and others like it, underscores the limitations of conventional Roman military tactics when confronted with a guerilla-style resistance, rooted in an intimate knowledge of the local environment and a fierce commitment to autonomy.

The enduring resistance of the Caledonian tribes also had a profound psychological effect on the Roman occupiers.

It instilled a grudging respect for their adversaries, influenced the Roman military strategy in the region, and contributed to the eventual decision to establish the frontier at Hadrian's Wall rather than pursue further expansion into the northern territories.

This outcome highlights the impact of local resistance on shaping the boundaries of one of history's greatest empires, a powerful reminder of the limitations of military and technological might when faced with determined opposition and challenging terrain.

Moreover, the interactions between Roman soldiers and the Caledonian tribes went beyond the battlefield, encompassing periods of trade, negotiation, and even cultural exchange.

These interactions, though often overshadowed by the narrative of conflict, played a significant role in shaping the frontier society.

They facilitated a degree of mutual understanding and accommodation, albeit within the asymmetrical power dynamics of occupier and occupied.

The legacy of these encounters, embedded in the archaeological record and the cultural memory of the region, offers a fascinating glimpse into the complexities of life on the edge of the Roman Empire.

In analyzing the military engagements between Roman forces and the Caledonian tribes, we gain not only a greater appreciation for the tactical ingenuity and resilience of the indigenous peoples of Britain but also a deeper insight into the adaptability and vulnerabilities of the Roman military system.

This exploration sheds light on the broader themes of imperial ambition, frontier dynamics, and the enduring power of local resistance, themes that resonate far beyond the specific historical context of Hadrian's Wall and the ancient conflicts of Roman Britain.

The examination of the Caledonian resistance against Roman expansion offers an invaluable lens through which to view the broader dynamics of power, identity, and landscape in ancient Britain.

The guerilla tactics employed by the Caledonian tribes, leveraging the formidable natural landscape of what is now Scotland, serve as a testament to the strategic acumen inherent in indigenous resistance movements.

This strategy not only confounded the Roman military apparatus but also compelled a reconsideration of the very nature of power and control in the ancient world.

The Romans, for all their engineering marvels and military discipline, found themselves ensnared in a terrain that defied conventional warfare.

The dense forests, steep hills, and boggy marshes of Caledonia became allies of the local tribes, concealing movements and providing natural fortifications that no Roman legion could easily overcome.

This environmental advantage was expertly exploited by the Caledonians, who conducted raids that struck swiftly from the shadows of the landscape, leaving little opportunity for the Roman forces to mount an effective counterattack.

In response to these challenges, the Roman military strategy evolved from direct confrontation to containment and surveillance.

The construction of Hadrian's Wall, and subsequently the Antonine Wall, can be interpreted as physical manifestations of this strategic shift.

These fortifications were not mere barriers but complex systems of control, incorporating forts, watchtowers, and gated milecastles designed to regulate movement and deter incursions.

Yet, the very necessity of these structures underscores the limitations of Roman power in the face of persistent guerilla resistance.

The Caledonian strategy also illuminates the role of leadership and collective identity in the resistance movement.

Figures such as Calgacus, traditionally celebrated in Roman accounts as a leader of the Caledonians at the Battle of Mons

Graupius, symbolize the unyielding spirit of defiance against imperial domination.

Whether myth or historical figure, Calgacus embodies the essence of Caledonian resistance—a fusion of individual valor and communal determination to preserve autonomy and identity against overwhelming odds.

This narrative of resistance and adaptation reveals the intricate dance between oppressor and oppressed, where power is contested not only on the battlefield but also in the realm of psychology, culture, and environmental mastery.

The Roman experience in Caledonia serves as a microcosm of imperial encounters across history, where technological and numerical superiority is often challenged by local knowledge, adaptability, and the indomitable will to resist.

In delving into these ancient conflicts, we uncover layers of human experience that resonate with contemporary struggles over territory, sovereignty, and identity.

The Caledonian resistance against Roman expansion is not just a historical episode but a chapter in the ongoing saga of human resilience and creativity in the face of external pressures.

It invites us to reflect on the enduring themes of conflict, adaptation, and the quest for autonomy that define the human condition.

Through this lens, Hadrian's Wall and the Antonine Wall transcend their roles as architectural feats, becoming symbols of the complex interplay between imperial ambition and local resistance.

These structures stand not only as remnants of a bygone era but as enduring monuments to the power of landscape, strategy, and the human spirit in shaping the course of history.

As we explore the multifaceted narratives of Roman Britain, we are reminded of the timeless nature of these themes and the lessons they hold for understanding the past and navigating the challenges of the present.

The narrative arc of Roman Britain, particularly as it pertains to the construction and legacy of Hadrian's Wall and the Antonine Wall, artfully encapsulates the perpetual tension between the forces of empire and the spirit of local resistance.

This dichotomy, a central theme of our exploration, not only shaped the historical landscape of ancient Britain but also offers profound insights into the human condition and the nature of power.

In this context, the walls transcend their initial military and administrative functions, rising as enduring symbols of this struggle.

Within the broader canvas of Roman imperial endeavors, the decision to erect these monumental barriers in the remote reaches of Britain reflects a nuanced understanding of governance, control, and human psychology.

The Romans, renowned for their military might and architectural ingenuity, recognized that true dominion over a territory extended beyond the mere subjugation of its people or the annexation of its land.

It required the establishment of a lasting presence, one that could command respect, instill order, and facilitate the integration of diverse cultures under the aegis of Roman rule.

Yet, the persistent defiance of the Caledonian tribes, coupled with the harsh and unforgiving landscape of northern Britain, presented a unique set of challenges to these imperial ambitions.

The construction of Hadrian's Wall, and later the Antonine Wall, can thus be seen as strategic responses to these challenges, embodying a sophisticated blend of military strategy, psychological warfare, and political symbolism.

These walls served not only to fortify the Roman frontier but also to demarcate the limits of Roman influence, both physically and ideologically.

They stood as tangible reminders of the empire's reach, signaling to both the Roman citizens and the indigenous populations the extent of Roman power and the boundaries of the civilized world as defined by Roman standards.

However, the legacy of these structures is not solely one of division and control.

Through the lens of history, they also reveal the complexities of cultural interaction and assimilation that occurred along the Roman frontier.

The presence of Roman garrisons and the establishment of trade routes facilitated a degree of economic and cultural exchange that blurred the lines between conqueror and conquered.

Local tribes adopted Roman customs, goods, and technologies, while Roman soldiers and settlers were influenced by indigenous practices and beliefs.

This exchange fostered a frontier culture that was both unique and transient, existing at the crossroads of two worlds.

The impact of this cultural synthesis extends beyond the immediate vicinity of the walls.

It contributed to the shaping of a distinct British identity, one that encompassed elements of both Roman and indigenous heritage.

This process of cultural fusion, while uneven and fraught with tension, underscores the capacity for human societies to adapt and evolve in the face of external pressures.

The walls, in this regard, function not only as historical artifacts but also as symbols of the dynamic interplay between cultures, the resilience of local identities, and the transformative power of empire.

In contemplating the historical significance of Hadrian's Wall and the Antonine Wall, it becomes clear that their importance lies not only in their physical remnants but in the stories they tell about the human experience.

These stories, woven from the threads of conflict, adaptation, and resilience, resonate with universal themes of identity, power, and resistance.

They invite us to reflect on the enduring legacy of the Roman occupation in Britain and its implications for our understanding of history and humanity.

Through a meticulous examination of these ancient frontiers, we gain not only a deeper appreciation for the ingenuity and ambition of the Roman Empire but also a profound understanding of the indomitable spirit of the peoples it sought to encompass.

The walls stand as monuments to the complexity of human endeavors, bearing witness to the intricate dance of conquest and coexistence that defines our shared past.

As we delve into the nuanced narratives of Roman Britain, we are reminded of the intricate web of factors that shape the course of history.

The construction of Hadrian's Wall and the Antonine Wall, far from being mere acts of military expediency, represent a confluence of strategic, cultural, and psychological factors that illustrate the complexities of imperial rule and the resilience of local cultures.

These ancient structures, in their enduring majesty and mystery, continue to captivate the imagination, offering timeless insights into the nature of civilization, the allure of empire, and the unyielding human drive for autonomy and identity.

Hadrian's Wall

Few structures embody the grandeur and the limitations of imperial ambition as poignantly as Hadrian's Wall. This edifice, a monumental testimony to the Roman Empire's vast reach, stands not just as a physical barrier but as a symbol of the ultimate failure to conquer the indomitable spirit of Scotland. Commissioned by Emperor Hadrian in 122 AD, it is believed to have taken six years to complete. The wall was constructed to mark the northern limit of Roman Britain and to defend the province from tribes living beyond the wall in what is now Scotland. The construction involved Roman soldiers, auxiliaries, and possibly local laborers. The wall stretched across what is now northern England, from the River Tyne near the North Sea to the Solway Firth on the Irish Sea, spanning approximately 73 miles (117 kilometers).

What if Hadrian's Wall was more than a mere fortification? What if its stones spoke not only of separation but also of a profound understanding and fear of the unknown? This provocation invites us to consider the wall not just as a physical barrier but as a complex symbol of cultural identity, psychological warfare, and political strategy.

The relevance of this question lies in the broader human tendency to erect boundaries, both literal and metaphorical. The construction of Hadrian's Wall, therefore, is not an isolated historical event but a lens through which we can explore the universal themes of division, security, and the dichotomy between 'us' and 'them.' Understanding why the Roman Empire, with its unparalleled military might and administrative prowess, resorted to building such an extensive boundary in a remote corner of their domain, sheds light on the complexities of human nature and governance.

The problem, at its core, involves examining the multifaceted reasons behind the wall's construction, which are often oversimplified as a straightforward military defense mechanism. This perspective fails to account for the intricate web of strategic, psychological, and political factors that influenced Roman decision-making. The challenges of maintaining a vast empire, the logistical nightmares of supplying remote outposts, the constant threat of rebellion, and the psychological impact of a 'barbarian' frontier on Roman soldiers and citizens alike were all critical elements in the calculus that led to the erection of Hadrian's Wall.

Common misconceptions about the wall often stem from a lack of appreciation for the complexity of these factors. Many view it simply as a failure of military strategy or as an admission of defeat, suggesting that Rome was unable to conquer the tribes of Scotland. Others romanticize it as a symbol of the Roman Empire's engineering prowess and administrative reach. While there is truth in these views, they overlook the subtler aspects of the wall's purpose and legacy, such as its role in controlling trade and migration, its function as a statement of power, and its impact on local populations.

Our unique approach involves a multidisciplinary analysis that synthesizes archaeological evidence, historical texts, and contemporary scholarship to paint a nuanced picture of Hadrian's Wall. By considering the wall from various angles—military, economic, psychological, and cultural—we aim to provide a more comprehensive understanding of its significance. This methodology allows us to appreciate the wall not merely as a relic of the past but as a reflection of timeless human drives and anxieties.

Illustrating this approach, we delve into the daily lives of the Roman soldiers stationed at the wall, the administrative challenges of sustaining such a remote frontier, and the interactions between Romans and local tribes. Through these lenses, we see the wall as a bustling hub of activity, a melting pot of cultures, and a focal point of conflict and cooperation. Moreover, by comparing Hadrian's Wall with other ancient and modern boundaries, we reveal common patterns in how societies attempt to manage their frontiers.

Anticipating skepticism, one might argue that focusing on such a wide range of factors complicates what was essentially a straightforward military endeavor. To this, we offer a counterargument: simplifying the narrative does an injustice to the complexity of human history and the intricate realities of empire-building. The Roman Empire's decision to construct Hadrian's Wall was not made in a vacuum but was the result of a multitude of strategic considerations, reflecting a deep understanding of the challenges and opportunities presented by their northern frontier.

In guiding the reader towards a deeper comprehension of these issues, we not only elucidate the past but also offer insights into contemporary debates surrounding borders, identity, and security. By examining the strategies employed by the Romans to manage their frontier, we gain valuable perspectives on the efficacy and ethics of modern boundary control measures. Additionally, by exploring the psychological and cultural dimensions of Hadrian's Wall, we encourage readers to reflect on the ways in which boundaries shape and reflect our understanding of ourselves and others.

In light of the above, it becomes imperative to dissect the concept of 'frontier' within the Roman imperial context, and to scrutinize how Hadrian's Wall fits into this intricate framework. The terms 'frontier', 'cultural identity', 'psychological warfare', and 'political strategy' emerge as critical to our discourse, each serving as a thread in the rich history that we endeavor to unravel. By delving into these terms, we aim to illuminate the multifaceted nature of Hadrian's Wall, transcending its physicality to explore its symbolic significance.

The term 'frontier' traditionally evokes images of a boundary separating civilized lands from the untamed wilderness. However, in the Roman context, it signified much more than a mere physical barrier; it represented the outermost edge of Roman influence, a zone of both conflict and cultural exchange. This nuanced understanding prompts us to consider the wall not just as a defensive structure, but as a dynamic interface between the Roman Empire and the indigenous peoples of Britain, where military, economic, and cultural interactions unfolded.

Turning our gaze to psychological warfare, we explore how Hadrian's Wall was instrumentalized as a tool of intimidation and control. Its sheer scale and permanence served as a tangible manifestation of Roman power, intended to demoralize the northern tribes and deter aggression. This aspect of the wall emphasizes the psychological underpinnings of Roman military strategy, revealing a sophisticated approach to conquest that extended beyond the battlefield to encompass the minds and spirits of their adversaries.

Political strategy, as it pertains to Hadrian's Wall, involves the calculated decisions behind its construction and maintenance, reflecting the Roman Empire's broader geopolitical ambitions. The wall was a statement of intent, a physical assertion of Rome's desire to consolidate its territory and project its authority to the edges of the known world. By analyzing the political motivations behind the wall, we gain insight into the imperial logic that dictated Roman expansion and consolidation strategies, offering a glimpse into the administrative and strategic genius that fueled their empire-building endeavors.

As we continue our exploration, we encourage you to ponder the intersections of these concepts in your understanding of Hadrian's Wall. How do these dimensions of frontier, psychological warfare, and political strategy converge to shape our perception of this ancient monument? In what ways do they illuminate the complexities of Roman frontier policy and its enduring legacy? By engaging with these questions, we delve deeper into the narrative of Hadrian's Wall, enriching our comprehension of its historical significance and the timeless lessons it imparts about the nature of boundaries, identity, and power.

In synthesizing these insights, we prepare to embark on a detailed examination of the wall's construction, its architectural and strategic features, and the daily lives of those who manned this frontier. This analysis will not only anchor our understanding of Hadrian's Wall in concrete historical realities but also elevate our appreciation for its symbolic resonance across centuries. As we traverse this historical landscape, we uncover the layers of human endeavor, resilience, and ingenuity encapsulated in this monumental boundary, drawing closer to the heart of what Hadrian's Wall represents in the saga of human civilization.

Turning our attention northwards, we encounter the Antonine Wall, a lesser-known but equally fascinating Roman frontier fortification in Britain. Constructed under the reign of Emperor Antoninus Pius, decades after Hadrian's Wall, this structure presents a unique case study for comparison and contrast. Began in 142 AD and finished in six years, its existence raises intriguing questions about the Roman Empire's shifting frontiers, the strategic reevaluations of its military doctrines, and the underlying motivations for its construction.

Unlike its more famous southern counterpart, the Antonine Wall was built primarily of turf on a stone foundation, stretching across the narrow neck of land between the Firth of Forth and the Firth of Clyde. This choice of materials and location speaks volumes about the practical and symbolic considerations that influenced Roman frontier policy. What does this divergence in construction technique and strategic positioning reveal about Roman intentions and capabilities at different points in their occupation of Britain?

In examining the parallels between these two monumental Roman works, we observe a shared purpose of demarcation and defense. Both walls served to delineate the boundary of Roman control, acting as physical and psychological barriers against the 'barbarian' north. They facilitated the projection of Roman power and the management of trade and migration, serving as checkpoints for the movement of goods and peoples. The presence of forts and watchtowers along both walls underscores their role as instruments of military surveillance and control, embodying the Roman approach to securing its frontiers.

However, the differences between Hadrian's Wall and the Antonine Wall are as telling as their similarities. The Antonine Wall's shorter span and less durable construction suggest a different level of commitment to the northern advance, possibly reflecting a more opportunistic or experimental approach to expansion under Antoninus Pius. Furthermore, the retraction back to Hadrian's Wall after a relatively brief occupation of the Antonine frontier highlights the challenges the Romans faced in controlling and assimilating the northern territories. This oscillation between expansion and consolidation offers rich insights into the dynamic nature of Roman frontier strategy and the limits of imperial ambition.

The implications of these observations extend far beyond the realm of ancient history. They prompt us to consider the factors that influence the rise and fall of empires, the fluidity of cultural boundaries, and the enduring legacy of ancient military and architectural endeavors. By comparing and contrasting Hadrian's Wall with the Antonine Wall, we gain a deeper understanding of the complexities involved in empire-building and frontier management.

Furthermore, this comparative study encourages us to reflect on the nature of historical memory and its impact on our interpretation of the past. The prominence of Hadrian's Wall in historical narratives and its physical preservation contrast sharply with the relative obscurity of the Antonine Wall, which has left a fainter imprint on both the landscape and the collective consciousness. This discrepancy raises questions about the factors that contribute to the preservation and commemoration of certain historical sites over others. How do these dynamics of memory and monumentality affect our understanding of history, and what can they teach us about the processes by which societies remember, honor, or forget their past?

In exploring the Antonine Wall as a counterpoint to Hadrian's Wall, we delve into a nuanced examination of Roman military strategy, architectural innovation, and the broader socio-political context of their time. This analysis not only enriches our understanding of Roman Britain but also invites us to consider the broader implications of frontier policies, the complexities of cultural exchange, and the legacies of ancient civilizations. As we unpack the layers of history embedded in these ancient walls, we uncover the enduring human themes of ambition, conflict, and the quest for security and identity in a changing world.

Let us now pivot our focus back towards the engineering marvel that is Hadrian's Wall, dissecting the construction techniques, logistics, and manpower that underscored Roman engineering prowess. The undertaking of building such a colossal structure across the rugged landscapes of Northern Britain was no small feat. It required not only architectural ingenuity but also a sophisticated understanding of logistics and manpower management.

The primary challenge in the construction of Hadrian's Wall was the geographical and environmental diversity of the terrain it spanned. From the craggy outcrops of the Whin Sill to the marshy lowlands near Solway Firth, each section of the wall presented unique obstacles. The implications of failing to effectively address these challenges were significant; it could compromise the wall's structural integrity and its effectiveness as a military fortification.

Without resolution, the wall risked becoming an expensive folly, a monument to overreach rather than a testament to the strategic acumen and engineering skill of the Roman Empire. Moreover, the logistical nightmare of transporting materials and provisions to remote construction sites could drain resources and demoralize the workforce, potentially stalling the project indefinitely.

The solution to this multifaceted problem was a testament to Roman engineering and administrative excellence. The Romans employed a segmented approach to construction, dividing the wall into sections and assigning each to a legion. This strategy allowed for simultaneous construction across multiple fronts, significantly accelerating the building process. Furthermore, by leveraging the local resources and adapting construction techniques to suit the specific demands of each terrain, the Romans minimized the logistical challenges.

For instance, in areas where stone was readily available, they constructed the wall using large blocks, ensuring durability and strength. In more remote or resource-scarce sections, they opted for turf and timber, materials that, while less durable, could be easily sourced and allowed for rapid progress. This adaptability in construction methods underscores the Romans' pragmatic approach to problem-solving.

The implementation of this grand project was not without its challenges. The harsh British weather, the difficulty of transporting materials across difficult terrain, and the constant threat of attacks from local tribes tested the resolve and ingenuity of the Roman builders. To mitigate these challenges, the Romans established a robust supply chain, utilizing both land and sea routes to ensure a steady flow of materials and provisions. Forts and smaller fortifications along the route provided protection for the workers and served as logistics hubs, facilitating the distribution of supplies.

The outcome of these efforts was a structure unparalleled in scale and sophistication for its time. Stretching across the width of Britain, Hadrian's Wall was not only a formidable military barrier but also a marvel of engineering, showcasing the Roman Empire's ability to mobilize and manage resources on an unprecedented scale. The wall's enduring legacy, evidenced by its remnants that still stand today, speaks to the success of the Roman approach to its construction.

In contrast, other solutions, such as a purely military conquest of the northern tribes or a reliance on natural barriers for defense, might have been less effective or sustainable in the long run. A military solution would have required a continuous and costly deployment of troops, while natural barriers could not provide the same level of control and surveillance as a constructed fortification.

The engineering prowess of the Romans, manifest in the construction of Hadrian's Wall, was complemented by an intricate system of milecastles and observation towers. These structures, spaced at regular intervals along the length of the wall, were pivotal in maintaining the security and efficiency of this frontier barrier. Their strategic placement and architectural design merit a closer examination, as they reveal the Romans' nuanced understanding of frontier defense and control.

Each milecastle was constructed at the interval of a Roman mile along the wall, serving as a gateway through this imposing barrier. These fortified gateways were not merely passageways but also acted as strongholds where soldiers could monitor and regulate the movement of people and goods across the frontier. The presence of such structures at regular intervals ensured that the wall could be effectively manned, with reinforcements readily available in the event of an attack or breach.

Observation towers, or turrets, were interspersed between the milecastles, typically at intervals of one-third of a Roman mile. These towers provided soldiers with elevated vantage points from which they could surveil the adjacent lands, keeping watch for potential threats. The strategic distribution of these towers along the wall facilitated a continuous line of sight across the frontier, significantly enhancing the Romans' ability to detect and respond to incursions swiftly.

The construction of milecastles and observation towers was informed by the same principles of adaptability and resourcefulness that characterized the broader project of Hadrian's Wall. Depending on the availability of materials and the specific demands of the terrain, these structures varied in size and construction materials. Some were built predominantly from stone, while others utilized timber and turf, reflecting the Romans' pragmatic approach to engineering challenges.

Inside the milecastles, accommodations for the garrisoned troops and storage facilities for supplies underscored the multifunctional nature of these fortifications. They were self-contained units that could support sustained military operations, underpinning the strategic depth of the Roman frontier defense system. The design of these structures, with their defensible gates and walls, exemplified the Romans' mastery of military architecture, marrying functionality with strategic necessity.

The interplay between milecastles and observation towers, each serving distinct yet complementary roles, illustrates the sophistication of Roman frontier management. This system did not rely solely on the passive barrier of the wall but integrated active defense mechanisms that could adapt to changing threats. It is a testament to the strategic acumen of the Roman military architects that these structures not only served their immediate defensive purposes but also facilitated the efficient administration of the frontier, controlling movement and trade in a manner that bolstered the economic and political aims of the empire.

Dawn of Departure

In 409 AD, one year after devistating attacks against them by Picts, Saxons and Scots, we find the Roman empires eviction from the shores of Britain. When we look at what caused this mighty empire to abandon its long reach, at least one question come to mind. What if the Roman departure from Britain was less a singular event and more a complex process, influenced by a confluence of factors both internal and external to the Roman Empire? This question invites us to delve deeper into the historical context, understanding not just the events themselves but their broader significance.

The importance of this inquiry lies not merely in the recounting of historical facts, but in the exploration of how the end of Roman rule in Britain serves as a microcosm for the challenges faced by empires in maintaining control over distant territories.

The problem at the heart of our exploration is multi-faceted, involving an intricate array of military, economic, and socio-political challenges that collectively undermined Roman authority in Britain. The military overextension of Rome, coupled with economic instability and the relentless pressure from barbarian invasions, highlights the complexity of the issue at hand.

These factors did not operate in isolation; rather, they were interlinked in a web of causality that precipitated the decline of Roman influence in Britain.

Common misconceptions about the Roman withdrawal often simplify these events into a narrative of military defeat or economic collapse. However, such interpretations overlook the nuanced reality of the situation.

The decline of Roman Britain was not merely the result of military incursions but was also deeply rooted in the economic turmoil and administrative challenges that beset the empire.

The failure to recognize the interconnectedness of these factors leads to an incomplete understanding of the historical dynamics at play.

Our unique approach to this complex issue is to examine it through a holistic lens, considering not only the immediate causes of the Roman withdrawal but also the underlying vulnerabilities that eroded the empire's capacity to maintain control over Britain.

By integrating military history with economic analysis and sociopolitical context, we offer a more nuanced understanding of the events leading up to the Roman departure.

This methodology allows us to appreciate the multifaceted nature of historical change, recognizing that the end of Roman rule in Britain was the culmination of a prolonged process of decline, rather than a sudden or isolated occurrence.

For instance, the Saxon Shore, a series of over nine fortifications along the southeastern coast of Britain along with extensive fortifications on the northern coast of Gaul, exemplifies the Roman response to the increasing maritime threats.

Yet, despite these defensive measures, Roman naval power was insufficient to secure the empire's extensive maritime borders.

This example underscores the limitations of military solutions in the face of broader structural challenges, illustrating the importance of considering economic and administrative capacities alongside military strategy.

In addressing potential objections to our approach, it is crucial to acknowledge the limitations of historical evidence and the inherent challenges in interpreting the past.

Skeptics may argue that the focus on economic and administrative factors detracts from the significance of military engagements in determining the course of history.

However, by presenting a balanced analysis that incorporates various perspectives, we aim to provide a comprehensive understanding of the complex forces that shaped the Roman withdrawal from Britain.

To apply this holistic perspective to the study of history, readers are encouraged to consider the interplay of economic, military, and socio-political factors in shaping historical events.

By examining the decline of Roman Britain through this integrated framework, we can gain insights into the broader patterns of historical change, enabling a deeper appreciation of the past and its implications for the present.

In doing so, we equip ourselves with the analytical tools necessary to navigate the complexities of historical interpretation, fostering a more nuanced and informed engagement with history.

In the preceding sections, we have laid the groundwork for understanding the multifarious factors that precipitated the Roman withdrawal from Britain. We now turn our attention to the structure and function of Roman governance in Britain, an examination essential for grasping the administrative underpinnings that both facilitated and foreshadowed the empire's eventual decline in this distant province.

Why, one might ask, is a detailed exploration of governance pivotal in this context? The answer lies in the revelation that the mechanisms of Roman control—encompassing legal, fiscal, and military domains—were not merely instruments of power but also barometers of the empire's health and efficiency. By dissecting these administrative facets, we can uncover the systemic weaknesses that rendered the empire vulnerable to both internal decay and external pressures.

Provincial Administration in Roman Britain was a complex network of local and imperial governance, designed to integrate the province into the wider empire while accommodating its unique characteristics. The Roman approach to provincial rule was both pragmatic and strategic, aiming to secure loyalty and facilitate economic exploitation through a combination of direct control and local autonomy. This dual strategy, however, was fraught with challenges, including the balancing act between empowering local elites and maintaining imperial authority, a dynamic that, over time, contributed to administrative inefficiencies and localized resistance.

Taxation and Economy, the lifeblood of the Roman state, were critical in sustaining the military and bureaucratic apparatus necessary for the control of vast territories such as Britain. The economic policies implemented in the province, including the levying of taxes in kind and coin, played a significant role in shaping the economic landscape. However, the fluctuating fortunes of the Roman economy, exacerbated by inflation, overreliance on slave labor, and the diminishing returns from conquests, increasingly strained the fiscal sustainability of the empire's governance model in Britain.

Military Governance in Roman Britain was characterized by a network of forts, roads, and military zones that facilitated rapid troop movement and reinforced Roman presence. The strategic distribution of military assets was pivotal in asserting control and deterring invasions. Yet, the military's role extended beyond mere defense; it was integral to the administration of justice, the maintenance of public order, and the implementation of infrastructure projects. The intertwining of military and civil governance, while effective in periods of stability, became a liability as the empire's military resources were stretched thin by external invasions and internal rebellions.

Through the prism of these defined terms, we embark on a narrative that not only recounts the decline of Roman authority in Britain but also illuminates the inherent vulnerabilities within the empire's governance structures. The exploration of provincial administration, taxation and economy, and military governance reveals a pattern of overextension, economic fragility, and administrative inefficiency, factors that, when combined with external pressures, precipitated the eventual withdrawal of Roman forces from Britain.

We see that the disintegration of Roman control in Britain was not merely the result of military defeats or economic crises in isolation but was symptomatic of deeper systemic issues that challenged the sustainability of Roman governance. This understanding allows us to appreciate the complexity of the empire's decline in Britain as a process rooted in both the internal dynamics of Roman administration and the external forces of change that reshaped the ancient world.

The exploration of Roman governance in Britain, with its focus on provincial administration, taxation, and military governance, sets the stage for a deeper understanding of the empire's eventual decline in this province. It is against this backdrop of administrative and economic fragility that we must consider the role of societal dynamics and cultural integration in the Roman experience in Britain.

The interplay between Roman settlers, native Britons, and subsequent invaders plays a crucial role in this historical narrative, highlighting the complexities of cultural assimilation and resistance that accompanied the administrative and military challenges facing the empire.

The societal dynamics in Roman Britain were marked by a fascinating blend of assimilation and coexistence, juxtaposed with periods of tension and conflict. Roman culture, law, and technology permeated British society, leaving an indelible mark on the social fabric of the province.

The construction of roads, baths, and public buildings, alongside the introduction of Latin language and Roman law, facilitated a degree of Romanization that shaped the identity of Britannia. However, beneath this veneer of cultural integration, there existed a persistent undercurrent of resistance and distinctiveness within the native population, which would, in time, contribute to the unique trajectory of Britain's post-Roman evolution.

The impact of cultural integration—or, in some cases, the lack thereof—on the administrative and military stability of Roman Britain cannot be overstated. The Roman approach to governance, which often sought to accommodate and incorporate local elites and customs, was a double-edged sword.

While it allowed for a measure of peace and cooperation, it also sowed the seeds for localized identities and loyalties that could, under the strain of economic and military pressures, turn against the imperial authority.

The delicate balance between Roman and native elements within Britain's societal framework was thus both a strength and a vulnerability, influencing the empire's capacity to respond to internal challenges and external threats.

Moreover, the arrival of new groups, such as the Saxons, Angles, and Jutes, in the wake of the Roman withdrawal, introduced additional layers of complexity to Britain's social landscape.

These groups brought with them their own customs, languages, and governance structures, which interacted with the remnants of Roman and native British elements in a dynamic process of cultural and political transformation.

However, the end of Roman rule did not signify a complete break with the past but rather the beginning of a process through which the foundations laid by the Romans were adapted, challenged, and reshaped by successive generations.

Dear Reader

As I conclude this introduction to the fascinating world of Roman Britain, I am filled with immense gratitude. Thank you for embarking on this exploration of history with me. It has been a privilege to delve into the rich history of Roman life in Britain and to share these stories and insights with you.

To the curious minds who followed along, I hope this journey has illuminated the past and brought it vividly to life. The history of Roman Britain is not just a narrative of conquest and governance; it's a tale of everyday life, resilience, and cultural exchange that shaped the course of this island's history.

I extend my heartfelt thanks to those who seek to understand the legacies left by the Romans and how they intertwined with the fabric of British society. Your interest and enthusiasm are the fuel that sustains the study of history and ensures that these stories continue to be told.

Lastly, I invite you to carry forward this knowledge and curiosity. Let us continue to explore the threads connecting our present to this rich and complex past. Together, we can uncover more of the secrets hidden beneath the earth and within the annals of time.

Thank you once again for joining me on this incredible journey. If you have enjoyed this book, we would love for you to leave a rating or review.

With warm regards,

History Nerds

Don't miss out!

Visit the website below and you can sign up to receive emails whenever History Nerds publishes a new book. There's no charge and no obligation.

https://books2read.com/r/B-A-ODOK-BELDD

BOOKS 2 READ

Connecting independent readers to independent writers.

Also by History Nerds

Ancient Empires
The Ottoman Empire
Rome: The Rise and Fall
The Mongol Empire
The Assyrian Empire
Ancient Egypt

Celtic Heroes and Legends
Celtic History
William Butler Yeats: Nobel Prize Winning Poet
Robert the Bruce
Scáthach
Finn McCool
William Wallace: Scotland's Great Freedom Fighter

Frauen des Krieges
Boudica: Königin der Icener
Jeanne d'Arc

Irena Sendler

Great Wars of the World
World War 1
World War 2
The Napoleonic Wars: One Shot at Glory
The Serbian Revolution: 1804-1835
Peace Won by the Saber: The Crimean War, 1853-1856
The American Civil War

Pirate Chronicles
Grace O'Malley: The Pirate Queen of Ireland
Blackbeard
William Kidd
Ching Shih
Anne Bonny

The History of England
Roman Britain
Medieval England
The Wars of the Roses
Tudor England

The History of the Vikings

Vikings
Longships on Restless Seas

Women of War
Boudica: Queen of the Iceni
Joan of Arc
Irena Sendler
Virginia Hall
Queen Amanirenas
Women of War Omnibus: Books 1-5

World History
The History of the United Kingdom
The History of Ireland
The History of America
The History of Scotland
The History of Wales
The History of India

Standalone
Grace O'Malley: Die Piratenkönigin von Irland

www.ingramcontent.com/pod-product-compliance
Lightning Source LLC
Chambersburg PA
CBHW021334160726

47994CB00007B/2688